Food and Energy:
Striking a Healthy Balance

KRISTIN PETRIE MS, RD
ABDO Publishing Company

visit us at
www.abdopublishing.com

Published by ABDO Publishing Company, 8000 West 78th Street, Edina, Minnesota 55439.
Copyright © 2012 by Abdo Consulting Group, Inc. International copyrights reserved in all
countries. No part of this book may be reproduced in any form without written permission from the
publisher. The Checkerboard Library™ is a trademark and logo of ABDO Publishing Company.

Printed in the United States of America, North Mankato, Minnesota.
062011
092011

 PRINTED ON RECYCLED PAPER

Cover Photos: Glow Images, iStockphoto
Interior Photos: Alamy p. 18; AP Images pp. 8, 15, 17; Corbis p. 25; Getty Images pp. 5, 11, 13, 29;
    iStockphoto pp. 1, 7, 23, 27; Neil Klinepier p. 15; US Department of Agriculture p. 21

Series Coordinator: BreAnn Rumsch
Editors: Megan M. Gunderson, BreAnn Rumsch
Art Direction: Neil Klinepier

Library of Congress Cataloging-in-Publication Data

Petrie, Kristin, 1970-
  Food and energy : striking a healthy balance / Kristin Petrie.
     p. cm. -- (Mission: Nutrition)
  Includes index.
  ISBN 978-1-61783-080-8
  1. Diet--Juvenile literature. 2. Food portions--Juvenile literature. 3. Nutrition--Juvenile literature.
I. Title.
  RA784.P4778 2012
  613.2--dc22
                                        2011012076

3246

Contents

Finding Balance

If you stop and listen, you'll probably notice someone telling you how to eat. Maybe your parents ask you to clean your plate. Or maybe they tell you not to eat too much! Some promise dessert if you finish your dinner. Others warn that eating certain foods will make you overweight.

These remarks seem to buzz around us constantly. Yet if you listen closely, they really don't make sense together. Some people say, "I'm on a diet" or "I'm bulking up." Others decide, "that's bad for you" or "that's good for you." With all these mixed messages, it's no wonder mealtime can be so confusing!

Food is an important part of daily life. Yet we constantly face questions about what, when, and how much to eat. So how do you make the right choices? How do you know what you are eating? And how do you know the right amount to eat? If you care about eating well, keep reading! You will find helpful answers to these common questions.

Eating for your health is a daily balancing act.

In and Out

Not only does food taste good, it is good for you. Food is also fun! You probably enjoy eating lunch with your buddies. You might also like helping your family make dinner. Food brings people together at meals, celebrations, and more.

Above all, food is our source of energy. After you eat, your body breaks down **nutrients** into glucose. This form of sugar provides your body with the fuel it needs. That energy is measured in **calories**. Every food you eat contains calories. And everything you do uses calories.

Kids ages 9 to 13 generally need to eat between 1,500 and 2,500 calories per day. Most kids do not need to keep track of their calories going in and out. Usually, making reasonable food choices and staying active is enough to keep you in balance.

Energy balance simply means that the energy you put in your body equals the energy that gets used. However, energy can become unbalanced over time. If you take in more energy than you use, you will gain weight. But if you use more energy than you take in, you will lose weight.

The actual number of calories you need depends on your age, size, and level of activity.

Now let's talk about how all that energy you feed your body gets used. A big chunk of your daily **calories** simply keeps your body ticking! They keep your heart pumping and your lungs breathing. They also keep your body running at the right temperature.

From thinking to running, everything you do requires calories. Even eating uses energy!

How many **calories** do you use up to fuel those basic body systems? That depends on your age, sex, and body size. The measure of how much energy you need for these functions is your basal metabolic rate (BMR). Everyone's BMR is different.

As long as your body is functioning, other calories provide you with energy for activity. The more active you are, the more energy you need! And the more energy you need, the more calories you will have to take in.

The amount of calories you burn during activity depends on how much you move. Your muscles, heart, and lungs need more energy to run than to walk. And they need more energy to play basketball than to watch the game on television.

This chart shows the energy a 75-pound (34-kg) child burns during common activities.

ACTIVITY LEVEL	ACTIVITY	CALORIES PER HOUR
resting	sleeping	30
very light	reading	35
light	walking	140
moderate	bicycling, dance practice	200
heavy	swim practice, basketball	250-350

Calorie Count

Okay, so you know you probably need between 1,500 and 2,500 **calories** per day. There are different ways to meet this need.

For example, you could eat five cups (1.25 L) of ice cream for around 2,000 calories. Yum! Unfortunately, ice cream consists mainly of fat. And too much fat can be unhealthy.

A better option would be to get your 2,000 calories from a bunch of different foods. Start the day with cereal, milk, and a banana. Munch on fruit and pretzels for a snack. Add a sandwich, veggies, and milk for lunch. Then, grab a yogurt after school. Later, have chicken, pasta, and a salad for dinner. You may even have a little room left for some of that ice cream!

The first option may sound more appealing. However, ice cream is loaded with empty calories. They deliver energy but few **nutrients**. Eating a variety of healthy foods will give you energy, vitamins, minerals, **protein**, **fiber**, and more. These are what your body needs to run well.

Chew On This

Empty calories add up fast! In fact, high-fat foods add up twice as fast as foods rich in protein or carbohydrates. This is because one gram (0.04 oz) of fat has nine calories. Protein and carbohydrates have just four calories per gram.

Smart Skills

How can you keep your energy balanced and your body working well? Stay active and make smart food choices. A few skills will help you practice this healthy lifestyle.

The first skill you need is simple. Pay attention to your body's signals. Eat when you are hungry, always starting with foods rich in **nutrients**. Stop eating when you are content. It takes your stomach 20 minutes to tell your brain you are full! So, eat slowly to see what it feels like to be satisfied, not stuffed.

This next skill is important, too. You need to listen to your thirst. Thirst is your body's way of telling you to **rehydrate**. Your body needs water to perform all its jobs properly. Did you know you lose about 10 cups (2.4 L) of water per day? This happens through sweating, urinating, and even breathing! So, you must replace this lost water each day to feel your best.

What's another important skill? Learn when you are hungry for something other than food. Sometimes you may feel like eating but don't know what you want. Emotions can make you feel this way. A change of activity or a talk with a friend may be what you're actually hungry for.

Sometimes you may think you are hungry when you are actually thirsty. Your body's signals can feel the same for these needs.

Decoding Labels

Thanks to your new skills, you know your growling tummy is telling you to eat! What to choose, what to choose? You want to make healthy choices. But how do you know what's in your food? With an apple or a carrot, it's pretty clear what you're getting. But what about a yogurt cup or a granola bar? What all is in there? Packaged foods can be mysterious.

Luckily, these foods have labels that list **nutrition** facts. The labels are there to take away some of the mystery. Nutrition facts include helpful information such as serving size, servings per container, and **calories** per serving.

Serving size is the recommended amount of a food that someone should eat. Servings per container is the number of servings in the package. Pay special attention to this number. It's easy to assume a food or beverage package holds just one serving. In reality, there may be two or more.

Calories per serving tells you how much energy a food provides in one serving. How do you know whether your food has a good

Freshest tasting within 5 days after opening.

Nutrition Facts

Serving Size 1 cup (240 mL)
Servings Per Container about 8

Amount Per Serving

Calories 130   Calories from Fat 45

	% Daily Value*
Total Fat 5g	8%
Saturated Fat 3g	15%
Trans Fat 0g	
Cholesterol 20mg	7%
Sodium 120mg	5%
Potassium 360mg	10%
Total Carbohydrate 12g	4%
Dietary Fiber 0g	0%
Sugars 11g	
Protein 8g	

Vitamin A 10%	•	Vitamin C 0%	
Calcium 30%	•	Iron 0%	
Vitamin D 25%			

* Percent Daily Values are based on a 2,000 calorie diet. Your daily values may be higher or lower depending on your calorie needs:

Calories:		2,000	2,500
Total Fat	Less than	65g	80g
Sat Fat	Less than	20g	25g
Cholesterol	Less than	300mg	300mg
Sodium	Less than	2,400mg	2,400mg
Potassium		3,500mg	3,500mg
Total Carbohydrate		300g	375g
Dietary Fiber		25g	30g
Protein		50g	65g

Calories per gram:
Fat 9   Carbohydrate 4   Protein 4

Fat reduced from 8g to 5g.

Ingredients: Organic Grade A Reduced Fat Milk, Vitamin A Palmitate, Vitamin D3.

From family farms near you, with regional distribution managed by Organic Valley, La Farge, WI 54639
1-888-444-MILK
www.organicvalley.coop

Oregon Tilth Certified Organic

Processed and packaged at plant stamped above.

✿ **Congratulations** for choosing products produced without antibiotics, synthetic hormones and persistent pesticides.

The number of servings you eat or drink affects all the label information that follows. Multiply your total servings by each nutrition fact to compute how much you actually had.

amount of **calories**? In general, a serving of 40 calories is low. Servings of 400 are high, and servings of 100 are average.

Next, the label lists major **nutrients**. These include fat, **protein**, and **carbohydrates**. The amounts included in each serving are usually measured in grams.

Your smarts about calories per gram comes in handy here! Do you remember that one gram (0.04 oz) of fat has 9 calories? So if a food lists 10 grams (0.4 oz) of fat, multiply 10 by 9. Now you know there are 90 calories from fat in that food. These calories should be limited.

The Daily Value (DV) percent is another handy tool. It helps you track the nutrients and calories in your diet. The numbers are based on an average diet of 2,000 calories.

Let's say that for breakfast, you have one serving of cereal. It provides 18 percent of your DV of carbohydrates. This means you have eaten 18 percent of the recommended carbs you need that day.

The DV also helps you see if foods are low or high in certain nutrients. If a food provides 20 percent DV or more, it is a good source. A food with 5 percent DV or less is a low source.

Last of all, the label includes a list of ingredients. This must be provided on all foods containing more than one ingredient. Ingredients are listed in the order of greatest weight. In addition, the list will say if a food includes **preservatives**, food coloring, and any major **allergens**.

Comparing food labels at the grocery store is a great way to make healthy choices.

Serving Sizes

Now you know how to find out what is in your breakfast cereal. The next step is to understand how much of it to eat. A simple experiment will show you why serving size is so important.

A serving is the recommended amount of a food. A portion is the amount you choose to eat.

Get two cereal bowls. Pour your usual amount of cereal into the first one. Then, use a measuring cup to pour one actual serving into the second bowl. The amount is shown on the label on the box. Now compare. Does the first bowl look the same as the second?

The portion you poured first may be smaller, about the same, or quite a bit larger than the second. In fact, most people eat more servings than they realize. Why does that matter? For **nutrition** information to be **accurate**, you must consider the actual amount eaten.

How do you know what makes one serving? You don't want to carry around measuring cups, right? If you know what a serving looks like, you will know how much you are eating. This is where tennis balls, playing cards, and other familiar objects come in handy. They are similar in size to servings of many foods.

Serving Sizes with Everyday Objects

FOOD	RECOMMENDED SERVING SIZE	VISUAL
dry cereal	1 cup (225 mL)	1 baseball
peanut butter	2 tablespoons (28 g)	1 golf ball
potato	1 medium	1 computer mouse
fresh vegetables	½ cup (118 mL)	½ baseball
apple or orange	1 medium	1 tennis ball
cheese	1½ ounces (43 g)	3 dominoes
meats and fish	2–3 ounces (57–85 g)	1 deck of cards or the palm of your hand

Balanced Foods

Now you know how to read food labels. You also know what a serving size is. But how do you know which foods to choose? And how much of each should you eat?

For kids who need an 1,800 **calorie** diet, the US Department of Agriculture (USDA) recommends 6 ounces (170 g) of grains a day. Aim for 2½ cups (568 mL) a day of vegetables and 1½ cups (343 mL) of fruits. You should also get 3 cups (750 mL) of dairy and 5 ounces (142 g) of **protein** each day.

Oils are not a food group, but they are still a part of a balanced diet. Those from olive oil, nuts, and fish have important health benefits. Fried foods, cookies, and chips contain less-healthy fats. They deliver empty calories, so eat them sparingly.

For many years, the USDA has provided Americans with advice and tools for keeping their diets balanced. In June 2011, it introduced a brand new tool called MyPlate.

MyPlate is an image of a place mat with a place setting on it. The plate is divided into four sections. Each represents one of four food groups. The cup, or bowl, represents the fifth food group.

MyPlate is a simple way to compare the USDA's advice to your own plate of food. Your plate should be half full of fruits and vegetables. Those foods should be paired with whole grains, lean **protein**, and low-fat dairy. One quick glance can tell you if your diet is balanced. It's that easy!

Did you notice what's missing? Fats and sugars are not a part of MyPlate. But, it is still okay to eat these on occasion. Just remember to build a healthy plate before enjoying treats.

Keeping Track

You've practiced your serving size smarts. And, you know how much you should get from each food group. What's next? Now you can have fun tracking your energy in.

There are many options for tracking what you eat. With a pen or pencil, jot down a note about that sandwich you ate. Draw the carrots that went with it. Write "moo" if you drank milk. Various online programs and tools can also add up what you eat. A good place to start is the USDA's MyPlate Web site.

Tracking your food doesn't have to be hard. It can be as simple as a memory. When you feel hungry, just picture what you've eaten so far that day. Have you covered all the food groups? Asking this question will help you make the best choice about what to eat next.

Tracking what you eat can be a helpful way to meet your energy needs. You can also plan for what to have next! Don't worry if your diet isn't perfect every day. Aim for the right amount and variety over the course of a few days.

Variety, balance, and moderation are three key messages for healthy eating. Check out www.choosemyplate.gov for more information!

Love Your Body

There's one thing left to understand about managing your energy balance. No two bodies look the same, whether they are in balance or not. Still, it can be hard to accept your body when comparing it to everybody else's.

Boys, you may wish you could gain weight and have big muscles. Until you reach **puberty**, your body is not able to make your muscles larger. In fact, lifting weights too early can injure growing bones, muscles, and joints. But you can still make your muscles stronger. Swimming, running, and playing are all great ways to build your strength.

Girls, you may feel pressure to be thinner or to develop curves. Your body will change a lot when you reach puberty. Don't turn to dieting, using weight loss products, or exercising too much. These are unhealthy ways to deal with your body's changes. Are you uncomfortable with your weight? Ask for help from a trusted adult or **nutrition** professional.

Use your smarts to feed your body well and stay active. Just remember, these efforts won't make you taller or thinner. And they definitely won't change your skin, hair, or eye color! But if you eat and exercise responsibly, your **unique** body will be just right.

Getting up and moving around is the best way to help your body stay fit without dieting.

Get Going!

When you're a kid, eating well and staying active may seem like a real pain. You probably like potato chips more than broccoli, right? And would you rather play video games than play outside? Maybe you even maintain a healthy weight without a balanced diet and exercise. So what's the point in changing?

The truth is, you may feel fine right now. But later, you most likely won't. Research shows the advantages of eating a well-balanced diet from an early age. For one, it reduces the risk of many adult health issues. These include heart disease and **diabetes**. Any adult will tell you, it's no fun to have these conditions slow you down.

Plus, living a healthy lifestyle today means you can enjoy its benefits now. Feed your body the foods it needs and keep it moving. Feel it thank you with more energy. You will run faster and play longer. Your brain will think better, and homework will seem easier!

Sound good? Then get going! Use your new knowledge and skills to create a healthy, balanced lifestyle. Your body will thank you now and later.

Healthy energy balance leads to a full and happy life!

A Healthier You

Today, many children in the United States face weight issues. Some are overweight or obese. Others struggle with unhealthy dieting. While this news is troubling, you now have the skills to feed your body well. Keep your energy in balance with these ideas from the *Let's Move!* program.

PORTION PERSPECTIVE! Control how much you eat with meals at home instead of in restaurants. Limit snacks and sugary drinks. You may be surprised to discover you still feel satisfied while eating less.

MOVE TOGETHER! Playing is always more fun with company. Encourage your family to join you for a hike or a game of kickball. You can also join activities offered by your community.

Let's Move!

For more information, check out *Let's Move!* online at **www.letsmove.gov**.

Let's Move! is a campaign started by First Lady Michelle Obama to raise a healthier generation of kids and combat childhood obesity. This movement works to provide schools, families, and communities with the tools to help kids be more active, eat better, and live healthfully.

The *Let's Move!* Web site provides information about the movement. It includes recipes as well as helpful tips on nutrition and physical activity. And, there are action tools to promote healthier foods in your local schools or start a *Let's Move!* Meetup.

COMPARE LABELS! Reading nutrition labels is just the beginning. The next step is to compare that information among similar products. This can help you eat foods packed with nutrients and avoid extra empty calories.

GET TALKING! Mealtime is also together time. Take the chance to visit about your day and share your feelings. Research shows that families who eat together tend to have healthier meals.

Index